Vijendra Singh
Shivani Pathak

Detecting Outliers: A Univariate Outlier and K-Means Approach

Vijendra Singh
Shivani Pathak

Detecting Outliers: A Univariate Outlier and K-Means Approach

LAP LAMBERT Academic Publishing

Imprint

Any brand names and product names mentioned in this book are subject to trademark, brand or patent protection and are trademarks or registered trademarks of their respective holders. The use of brand names, product names, common names, trade names, product descriptions etc. even without a particular marking in this work is in no way to be construed to mean that such names may be regarded as unrestricted in respect of trademark and brand protection legislation and could thus be used by anyone.

Cover image: www.ingimage.com

Publisher:
LAP LAMBERT Academic Publishing
is a trademark of
International Book Market Service Ltd., member of OmniScriptum Publishing Group
17 Meldrum Street, Beau Bassin 71504, Mauritius

ISBN: 978-3-659-39184-2

Zugl. / Approved by: MITS University, 2013

Detecting Outliers:

A

Univariate Outlier and K-Means Approach

Mr. Vijendra Singh
Ms. Shivani Phatak

Faculty of Engineering and Technology
Mody Institute of Technology and Science
(Deemed University Under Section 3 of the UGC Act 1956)
Lakshmangarh-332311 (Dist.-Sikar)

TABLE OF CONTENTS

ABSTRACT

Outlier detection is a fundamental issue in data mining, specifically it has been used to detect and remove anomalous objects from data. Outliers are generally those points which are different from or inconsistent with the rest of the data. Novel, new, abnormal, unusual or noisy information can all be called outliers. Sometimes the outliers are more interesting than the majority of the data, such as the applications of intrusion detection and unusual usage of credit cards. With the increase of the complexity and variety of datasets, the challenges of outlier detection are how to catch similar outliers as a group, and how to evaluate the outliers. The research described in this dissertation has investigated the above challenges and has addressed the solutions.

Firstly, this thesis presents a theoretical overview of outlier detection approaches. An integrated outlier detection method is proposed and analyzed, which is named *"Detecting Outliers: A Univariate Outlier and K-Means Approach"*. It provides efficient outlier detection and data clustering capabilities in the presence of outliers, and based on filtering of the data after univariate analysis. The algorithm of our outlier detection method is divided into two stages. The first stage provides *Univariate outlier analysis.* The main objective of the second stage is an iterative removal of objects, which are far away from their cluster centroids by applying K-means algorithm. The removal occurs according to the minimisation of the value of sum of the distances of all the points to their respective centroid in all the clusters. Finally, we provide experimental results from the application of our algorithm on several datasets to show its effectiveness and usefulness. The empirical results indicate that the proposed method was successful in detecting outliers and promising in practice.

ACKNOWLEDGEMENS

It is our profound privilege to express our deep sense of gratitude towards our institute Faculty of Engineering and Technology, Mody Institute of Technology and Science, Lakshmangarh. We would like to thank Dean FET Dr. P. K. Das and HOD CSE for providing us with the required facilities, better environment and cooperation without which the completion of the work would not have been possible.

Finally, we thank and owe my deepest regards to all of them and all others who have helped us directly or indirectly in making this dissertation a success.

Ms. Shivani Pathak
Mr. Vijendra Singh

LIST OF FIGURES

LIST OF TABELS

CHAPTER 1

INTRODUCTION

In this decade, we have seen a widespread use of data mining applications by universities, industries and business organizations. The data mining applications are used to discover the behaviors of the collected observations, which could have not been found manually. The corporations utilize this knowledge to gain a competitive advantage by being able to predict the market and user behaviors more accurately. The government uses data mining methods to detect fraudulent activities. Research institutions apply data mining methods to better understand the relationships in the dataset that may lead to scientific discovery. Generally, data mining is used to infer the common patterns in a data set. The common techniques are association rule mining, clustering and classification. However, recently, along with pattern detection, the data mining community is showing substantial interest in detecting outliers in datasets.

1.1 Basic Definition of Outlier

Outlier detection is one of the basic problems of data mining. An outlier is an observation of the data that deviates from other observations so much that it arouses suspicions that it was generated by a different mechanism from the most part of data [1]. Novel, new, abnormal, unusual, noisy or erroneous information can all be called outliers. Outliers are those points which are different from or inconsistent with the rest of the data [2]. Novelty detection [3], chance discovery [4], and anomaly detection are different names for outlier detection. Inliers, on the other hand, are defined as an observation that is explained by underlying probability density function. This function represents probability distribution of main part of data observations. Outliers may be erroneous or real in the following sense. Real outliers are observed whose actual values are very different than those observed for the rest of the data and violate plausible relationships among variables. Erroneous outliers are observations that are distorted due to misreporting or misrecording errors in the data-collection process. Outliers of either type may exert undue influence on the results of statistical analysis, so they should be identified using reliable detection methods prior to performing data analysis [5].

1

1.1.1 Outlier from Statistics Point of View

According to a definition given by Hawkins "An outlier is an observation which deviates so much from the other observations as to arouse suspicions that it was generated by a different mechanism". Statistics-based intuition behind this is "Normal data objects follow a "generating mechanism", e.g. some given statistical process and abnormal objects deviate from this generating mechanism". We present here a well known example of outlier to explain our point better.

Example: Hadlum vs. Hadlum

- The birth of a child to Mrs. Hadlum happened 349 days after Mr. Hadlum left for military service.
- Average human gestation period is 280 days (40 weeks).
- Statistically, 349 days is an outlier.

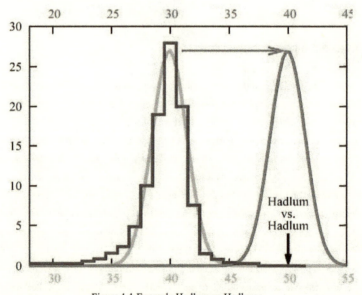

Figure 1.1 Example Hadlum vs Hadlum

In figure 1.1 blue lines are statistical basis (13634 observations of gestation periods) green lines are assumed underlying Gaussian process. Very low probability for the birth of Mrs. Hadlums child for being generated by this process. Red line is the assumption of Mr. Hadlum (another Gaussian process responsible for the observed birth, where the gestation period starts later). Under this assumption the gestation period has an average duration and the specific birthday has highest possible probability.

1.2 Challenges with Outlier Detection

A key challenge in outlier detection is that it involves exploring the unseen space. As mentioned earlier, at an abstract level, an outlier can be defined as a pattern that does not conform to expected normal behavior. A straightforward approach will be to define a region representing normal behavior and declare any observation in the data which does not belong to this normal region as an outlier. But several factors make this apparently simple approach very challenging.

- Defining a normal region which encompasses possible normal behaviour is very difficult.
- Often time's normal behavior keeps evolving and an existing notion of normal behavior might not be sufficiently representative in the future.
- The boundary between normal and outlying behavior is often fuzzy. Thus an outlying observation which lies close to the boundary can be actually normal and vice versa.
- The exact notion of an outlier is different for different application domains. Every application domain imposes a set of requirements and constraints giving rise to a specific problem formulation for outlier detection.
- Availability of labelled data for training/validation is often a major issue while developing an outlier detection technique.
- In several cases in which outliers are the result of malicious actions, the malicious adversaries adapt themselves to make the outlying observations appear like normal, thereby making the task of defining normal behavior more difficult.
- Often the data contains noise which is similar to the actual outliers and hence is difficult to distinguish and remove.

1.3 Outlier Detection in Data

Historically, outliers have been studied extensively in statistics especially for discarding of noise. Those unwelcome errors will affect the observations and contaminate the computation results. The outliers can be detected by conducting hypothesis tests, e.g. Grubb's test or performing univariate or multivariate analysis. New requirements have changed people's attitudes toward outliers. Outlier detection cannot be limited by statistics. Especially, with the increase of the complexity and variety of the dataset, the new challenges of outlier detection have higher requirement of outlier detection algorithms. In several applications, analysts will likely have interest in investigating the outliers. Univariate analysis can be performed on the single attribute while the multivariate analysis is performed on a group of attributes. Outliers can also be detected as a by product of clustering algorithms. Clustering algorithms forms a separate cluster of the points which are deviated from the other points. In case of univariate outliers a single attribute is tested for the presence of outlier, so the outliers present in that particular attribute can be detected by univariate analysis. But it usually doesn't tell us anything about the impact of the outlier on the data.

Our contribution in the thesis is to have the knowledge about the outlier values in the data using univariate outlier detection as a pre-processing task and then to check the impact of those outliers we use k-means algorithm, by this we calculate the value of sum of all points to centroid distance in every cluster. Our objective is to minimise the value of sum. If outlier values increases the value of sum we will delete those entries from the data. Hence the algorithm presented here, provides an integration of Univariate outlier detection and k-means algorithm to detect and calculate the impact of those outliers. To ignore the problem of local minima in k-means clustering we used 'iterations' to optimize the value of sum. We integrated two different approaches so as to overcome the short comings of both the approaches if used separately.

1.4 Practical Applications

Outlier detection has been a widely researched problem and finds immense use in a wide variety of application domains such as credit card, insurance, tax fraud detection, intrusion detection for cyber security, fault detection in safety critical systems, military surveillance for

4

enemy activities and many other areas. The importance of outlier detection is due to the fact that outliers in data translate to significant (and often critical) information in a wide variety of application domains. For example, an anomalous traffic pattern in a computer network could mean that a hacked computer is sending out sensitive data to an unauthorized destination. In public health data, outlier detection techniques are widely used to detect anomalous patterns in patient medical records which could be symptoms of a new disease. Similarly, outliers in credit card transaction data could indicate credit card theft or misuse. In handwritten word recognition some errors were caused by non-character images that were assigned high character confidence value. Segmentation and dynamic programming (DP)-based approaches are used for outlier rejection in off-line handwritten word recognition method. The flow diagram is shown in Figure.1.2 Segmentation splits a word image into partial characters than use character classifier and DP to obtain the optimal segmentation and recognition result. The recognition process assigns a match score to each candidate string and the highest score determines the result. The focus of this approach is to assign low character confidence values to non-character images, which means to reject outlier. The neural networks were used to realize outlier rejection, where valid patterns only activate the output node corresponding to the class, which the pattern belongs to. Outliers do not activate any output node [23].

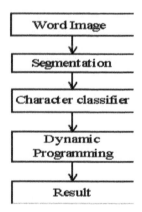

Figure.1.2. Diagram of handwritten word recognition system.

1.5 Organization of the Thesis

This report is organized as follows. In the Chapter 2, we will present important research in outlier detection as related work. In the Chapter 3, we will discuss the proposed method to detect and analyse the outlier and their effect on the data. Chapter 4 presents the experimental results of the proposed method using two different datasets Fisheriris and GSS93. Chapter 5 describes the conclusion and the future work.

CHAPTER 2

RELATED WORK

Hodge & Austin [8] gave a survey of outlier detection methods, focusing especially on those developed within the Computer Science community. Supervised outlier detection methods require pre-labelled data, tagged as normal or abnormal, and are suitable for data whose characteristics do not change through time. In semi-supervised recognition methods, the normal class is taught, and data points that do not resemble normal data are considered outliers. Unsupervised methods process data with no prior knowledge. We describe different approaches to detect the outliers. Four important categories of unsupervised outlier detection algorithms are (1) In a clustering-based method, like ROCK (a robust clustering algorithm for categorical attributes) [6], DBSCAN (a density-based algorithm for discovering clusters in large spatial databases) [9], partitional clustering outliers are by-products of the clustering process and will not be in any resulting cluster. (2) The density-based method of [10] and [14] uses a Local Outlier Factor (LOF) to find outliers. If the object is isolated with respect to the surrounding neighbourhood, the outlier degree would be high, and vice versa. (3) The distribution-based method [13] defines, for instance, outliers to be those points p such that at most 0.02% of points are within 0.13σ of p. (4) Distance-based outliers are those objects that do not have "enough" neighbours [11]. The problem of finding outliers can be solved by answering a nearest neighbour or range query centred at each object O. A novel approach named ABOD (Angle-Based Outlier Detection) and some variants assessing the variance in the angles between the difference vectors of a point to the other points. This way, the effects of the "curse of dimensionality" are alleviated compared to purely distance-based approaches. A main advantage of this new approach is that our method does not rely on any parameter selection influencing the quality of the achieved ranking. In a thorough experimental evaluation, ABOD is compared to the well-established distance-based method LOF [15]. Several mathematical methods can be applied to outlier detection. A comparison of different techniques is given in [34]. Wavelets may be used to transform the original feature space, and then find dense regions in the transformed space. A wavelet transform decomposes a signal into different frequency sub bands. By using low-pass filters, a wavelet transform can detect outliers [18]. Principal component analysis (PCA) may also be used to detect outliers.

7

PCA computes orthonormal vectors that provide a basis for the input data. Then principal components are sorted in order of decreasing "significance" or strength. The size of the data can be reduced by eliminating the weaker components which are with low variance [17]. The convex hull method finds outliers by peeling off the outer layers of convex hulls [16]. Data points on shallow layers are likely to be outliers. Our algorithm is an unsupervised outlier detection method. This dissertation focuses on this type of algorithm for comparison and analysis.

2.1 Proximity-Based Approaches

Examine the spatial proximity of each object in the data space If the proximity of an object considerably deviates from the proximity of other objects it is considered an outlier. Sample approaches are Distance based approaches; Density based approaches, Subspace outlier detection approaches.

2.1.1 Density-Based Algorithm

M. Breunig created an outlier detection algorithm based on an object's neighbourhood density, i.e. estimating the density at point p by analyzing its k nearest neighbours. By measuring the difference in density between an object and its neighbouring objects, this algorithm assigns every object a degree of being an outlier called Local Outlier Factor (LOF) [33]. If the object is isolated with respect to the surrounding neighbourhood, the LOF value would be high, and vice versa.

The outlier detection processes are as follows. First, the algorithm finds every object's k nearest neighbors. Then, reachability distance of an object p w.r.t. object o filters out small changes of reachability distance in a uniform density area. For points far away, reachability distance is the original distance from o to p, written $d\ (p,\ o)$; for points within the kth neighborhood, reachability distance is taken as the distance to the kth nearest neighbor of o, written k-distance (o)(eq. 2.1). Thus, it smoothes small differences in uniform areas. The algorithm has a single parameter MinPts, i.e., the number of an object's nearest neighbors. When MinPts changes from low to high, an outlier's LOF value may change substantially. The objects with high LOF values are outliers.

$$reachDistk \; (p,o) = \max \; \{ \; d \; (p, o) \; , \; k\text{-}distance(o) \; \} \qquad (2.1)$$

From LOF Formulas, we can see, on one side, each node's LOF value does reflect the outlier ability: adding one point p' near the outlier p will decrease reachability distance and increase the reachability density (lrdMinPts(p)), decrease the value $LOF(p)$,and decrease the outlier degree of p (Figure 2.1 (a)); adding one point p' near the cluster (neighbors) that p is outlying will decrease reachabilty distance and increase the reachability density lrdMinPts(o)) , increase the value $LOF(p)$, and increase the degree of outlier p (Figure 2.1 (b)). On the other side, LOF could hide outliers because of the value of parameter $MinPts$.

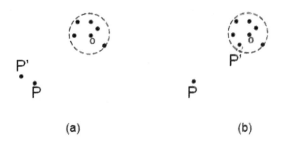

P'

P

P'

P

(a)   (b)

Figure.2.1. MinPts and Neighbors (a) adding a point p' near to the outlier p. (b) adding a point p' near to the cluster p is outlying.

2.1.2 Distribution-Based Algorithm

Inspired by statistical methods of defining outliers, Knorr and Ng proposed the following as a unified definition of outliers: "An object O in a dataset T is a UO (p, D)-outliers if at least fraction p of the objects in T is at least distance D from O." Although no standard distribution can adequately model the observed distribution, the purpose here is to fit the observed distributions into standard distributions. For a suitable partition p and distance D, if an object O is an outlier according to a specific discordance test, the O is also a UO(p, D)-outlier. They gave the outlier definition for the normal distribution. Outliers can be considered to be points that lies 3 or more standard deviations (σ) from the mean. T is an outlier according to Def. Normal iff *t* is a UO (0.9988, 0.13σ)-outlier.

2.1.3 Distance-Based Algorithm

The authors who developed the distribution-based method created distance-based outlier detection algorithms They define a point *O* to be a *DB* (p, D)-outlier (where *D* is a distance and $0 \leq p \leq 1$) if at least M (M=N*p, N is the dataset size) neighbours lie greater than distance *D* from *O*. The difference between this algorithm and the distribution-based method is that it is suitable for situations where the dataset does not fit any standard distribution. The problem of finding all *DB* (*p, D*)-outliers can be solved by answering a nearest neighbor or range query centered at each object *O*. More specifically, based on a standard multidimensional indexing structure, such as r-tree or kd-tree, the algorithm executes a range search with radius *D* for each object *O*, i.e. for each object *O* it searches for all objects within distance *D* from *O*. If more than *M* (*M* = N*(1-p)) neighbours are found in the *D*-neighbourhood, *O* is not an outlier. Knorr and Ng relied on the computation of distance values based on a metric distance function. The algorithm assumed the distance function is (weighted) Euclidean and claimed the two above approaches are for any k-dimensional datasets.

2.1.4 Sub-Space Based Outlier Detection

Model for subspace based clustering is given by Kriegel in 2009, motivation for this was Outliers may be visible only in subspaces of the original data. The steps for performing the outlier check are-

- Compute the subspace in which the *k*NNs of a point *p* minimize the variance
- Compute the hyperplane H (*kNN* (*p*)) that is orthogonal to that subspace.
  - Take the distance of *p* to the hyperplane as measure for its "outlierness"

2.2 Model-Based Approaches

Apply a model to represent normal data points. Outliers are points that do not fit to that model. Sample approaches are probabilistic tests based on statistical models, Depth-based approaches, Deviation-based approaches and some subspace outlier detection approaches. Here is a brief introduction of all of them.

2.2.1 Depth-Based Approach

Depth-based approaches search for outliers at the border of the data space but independent of statistical distributions. It organizes data objects in convex hull layers. Outliers are objects on outer layers. Basic assumptions are outliers are located at the border of the data space and normal objects are in the center of the data space,as shown in the figure 2.2

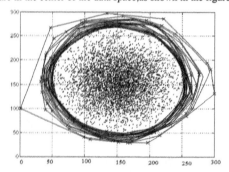

Figure 2.2 Convex Hull Layers of Data

There is a well known model of depth based approach given by Tukey, he stated that Points on the convex hull of the full data space have depth = 1, Points on the convex hull of the data set after removing all points with depth = 1 have depth = 2 and the points having a depth $\leq k$ are reported as outliers, as shown in the figure 2.3.

11

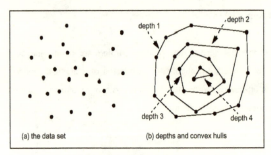

Figure 2.3 Depth Based Approach

2.2.2 Deviation-Based Approach

Deviation based approaches assumes that Outliers are the outermost points of the data set. Given a set of data points (local group or global set) outliers are points that do not fit to the general characteristics of that set, i.e., the variance of the set is minimized when removing the outliers. A known model was given by Arning, he stated that given a smoothing factor SF(I) that computes for each $I \subseteq DB$ how much the variance of DB is decreased when I is removed from DB-

  – If two sets have an equal *SF* value, take the smaller set

  – The outliers are the elements of the exception set $E \subseteq DB$ for which the following holds:

$$SF\ (E) \geq SF\ (I)\ \text{for all}\ I \subseteq DB$$

It have a similar idea like classical statistical approaches (k = 1 distributions) but independent from the chosen kind of distribution, here heuristics like random sampling or best first search are applied. It can be applicable to any data type (depends on the definition of SF) and is originally designed as a global method, which outputs a labelling.

2.3 Angle-Based Approaches

Examine the spectrum of pairwise angles between a given point and all other points. Outliers are points that have a spectrum featuring high fluctuation. This approach is further previous in this chapter

2.4 Cluster-Based algorithms

Halkidi et al. reviewed different clustering algorithms. Some of the clustering algorithms[35], such as k-means, put every object in a cluster and cannot handle exceptions. In this case, outliers can greatly influence the clustering results. For those clustering algorithms which are robust with outliers, outliers are a by-product of the clustering process and those outliers will not be in any clusters. We call a clustering algorithm robust if it attempts to identify outliers while performing clustering. Because the main objective of clustering algorithm is to find clusters, the notions of detected outliers are binary and do not have quantification measures.

2.4.1 Clustering Problems

The general clustering problem includes three subproblems: (i) selection of the evaluation function; (ii) decision of the number of groups in the clustering; and (iii) the choice of the clustering algorithm [25][34].

2.4.2. Evaluation of Clustering

An objective function is used for evaluation of clustering methods. The choice of the function depends upon the application, and there is no universal solution of which measure should be used. Commonly used a basic objective function is defined as (2.2):

$$f(P,C) = \sum_{i=1}^{n} d(x_i, c_{p_i})^2 , \qquad (2.2)$$

where P is partition and C is the cluster representatives, d is a distance function. The Euclidean distance and Manhattan distance are well-known methods for distance measurement, which are used in clustering context. Euclidean distance is expressed as (2.3):

$$d(x_1, x_2) = \sqrt{\sum_{i}^{k} (x^i_1 - x^i_2)} , \qquad (2.3)$$

13

and Manhattan distance is calculated as (2.4):

$$d(x_1, x_2) = \sum_1^k \left| x'_1 - x'_2 \right|,$$ (2.4)

2.4.3 Number of Clusters

The choice of number of the clusters is an important sub-problem of clustering. Since a priori knowledge is generally not available and the vectors dimensions are often higher than two, which do not have visually apparent clusters. The solution of this problem directly affects the quality of the result. If the number of clusters is too small, different objects in data will not be separated. Moreover, if this estimated number is too large, relatively regions may be separated into a number of smaller regions. Both of these situations are to be avoided. This problem is known as the cluster validation problem. The aim is to estimate the number of clusters during the clustering process. The basic idea is the evaluation of a clustering structure by generating several clustering for various numbers of clusters and compares them against some evaluation criteria. In general, there are three approaches to investigate cluster validity [27]. In *external* approach, the clustering result can be compared to an independent partition of the data built according to our intuition of the structure of the dataset. The *internal criteria* approach uses some quantities or features inherent in the dataset to evaluate the result. The basic idea of the third approach, *relative criteria*, is the evaluation of a clustering structure by comparing it to other clustering schemes, produced by the same algorithm but with different input parameter values. The two first approaches are based on statistical tests and their major drawback is their high computational cost. In the third approach aim is to find the best clustering scheme that a clustering algorithm can define under certain assumptions and parameters. The following clustering algorithms are robust with outliers.

2.4.4 ROCK

ROCK is a hierarchical clustering algorithm for Boolean and categorical attributes data. ROCK uses links to measure the similarities between objects instead of distances. The number of links between a pair of points is then the number of common neighbours for the points. Points belonging to a single cluster will in general have a large number of common neighbours, and consequently more links. Thus, during clustering, merging clusters/points with the most number of links first will result in better and more meaningful clusters. ROCK is robust with regard to outliers. The similarityθ is the threshold for outliers. For points with low similarity with other points (less thanθ), they do not have similar neighbours, so they do not have common neighbours (links) with other points. Points below the similarity will not attend the merging process for finding clusters. For ROCK, outliers are the points with low similarities with other points.

2.4.5 DBSCAN

DBSCAN (Density-Based Spatial Clustering of Applications with Noise) is a density-based clustering algorithm. A core object contains a minimum number, MinPts, of objects, within an e-neighbourhood. For a given set of objects, D, we say that an object p is directly density-reachable from object q if p is within the e-neighbourhood of q, and q is a core object. DBSCAN is based on these definitions. DBSCAN searches for clusters by checking the e-neighbourhood of each point in the database. If the e-neighbourhood of a point p contains more than MinPts, a new cluster with p as a core object is created. Density-based DBSCAN then iteratively collects directly density-reachable objects from these core objects, which may involve the merge of a few density-reachable clusters. The process terminates when no new point can be added to any cluster. Objects not contained in any cluster are considered to be outliers.

2.4.6 Clustering Application

Clustering problems are widely used in numerous applications, such as customer segmentation, classification, and trend analysis. For example, consider a retail database records containing items purchased by customers. A clustering procedure could group the customers in such a way that customers with similar buying patterns are in the same cluster [26]. Many real word applications deal with high dimensional data. It has always been a challenge for clustering algorithms because of the manual processing is practically impossible [24]. A high quality computer-based clustering removes the unimportant features and replaces the original set by a smaller representative set of data objects. As a result, the size of data reduces and, therefore, cluster analysis can contribute in compression of the information included in data. Cluster analysis is applied for prediction. Suppose, for example, that the cluster analysis is applied to a dataset concerning patients infected by the same disease. The result is a number of clusters of patients, according to their reaction to specific drugs. So, for a new patient, we identify the cluster in which he can be classified and based on this decision his medication can be made [26].

2.5 Mathematical Outlier Detection Algorithms

Several mathematical methods can be applied to outlier detection. Wavelets may be used to transform the original feature space, and then find dense regions in the transformed space. A wavelet transform decomposes a signal into different frequency sub bands. By using low-pass filters, a wavelet transform can detect outliers. Principal component analysis (PCA) may also be used to detect outliers. PCA computes orthonormal vectors that provide a basis for the input data. Then principal components are sorted in order of decreasing "significance" or strength. The size of the data can be reduced by eliminating the weaker components which are with low variance. The convex hull method finds outliers by peeling off the outer layers of convex hulls. Data points on shallow layers are likely to be outliers.

2.6 Statistical Outlier Detection Algorithms

Outlier detection, both univariate and multivariate, has long been a concern of statistics. Barnett and Lewis gave a review of outliers in statistical data. They thought "...more fundamentally, the concept of an outlier must be viewed in relative terms." "Relative terms" means that outliers are declared by subjective judgments. They described outliers in different situations and classified outlier problems into four categories:

- Human errors and mistakes. Wrong records or presentations of data are a common type of outliers. Outliers caused by human mistakes are not related to statistical factors. Discarding is usually the way to deal with this type of outliers.
- Outliers in probability models. A probability distribution is found to fit the majority or overall data. Outliers are identified relatively to the distribution.

- Outliers in structured situations. Regression models and time series data are the two most discussed models. Outliers are an important source of trouble when performing regression. Outliers are those observations that present obvious discrepancy in relation to the model. Regression outlier detection methods include linear least square, R-student, Cook's D etc.
- Decision analysis. Barnett (1994) gave a comprehensive introduction about decision theory and statistical inference. Decision analysis needs to consider outliers. The book stressed Bayesian methods, which are conventional decision making methods to make decisions, and can also detect outliers.

Barnett and Lewis's introduction to outliers is from the statisticians' view. Their recognition methods and classification of outliers are different from Hodge and Austin, who are from computer science. Besides classification into supervised, semi-supervised and unsupervised problems, Hodge and Austin introduced four types of solution method: statistical models, neural networks, machine learning and hybrid systems. Neural networks are for decision analysis. Machine learning methods are especially for categorical data. Decision trees and SVM (support vector machines) are among this type of outlier detection method. Hybrid systems combine technologies from different areas and try to overcome their weaknesses and handle all situations. PAELLA designs a mixture model which combines the EM (Expectation Maximization) algorithm, clustering analysis and Mahalanobis distance and detects for both normal and non-normal multivariate data sets. Hodge and Austin classified the statistical models into four categories:

- Proximity-based techniques. This type of technique is independent of the distribution. The complexity is related to the dimension and size of the data. Methods using k-nearest neighbours and distance calculations are this type of outlier detection algorithm. The distribution-based and distance-based methods we introduced at the beginning of this chapter are both proximity-based techniques. For example, Mahalanobis distance can point out outliers in both univariate and multivariate data, and several more robust methods are described. Clustering algorithms using k-medoids, such as CLARANS and PAM (Partition around Medoids) are in this category too.

- Parametric methods. This type of method is good for large datasets. The complexity is decided by the models not data size. Regression methods, PCA, SVM, and EM (expectation maximization) are all in this class. Hodge and Austin also consider the convex hull method to be a parametric method.
- Non-parametric methods. This type of method is for models whose distribution is known.
- Semi-parametric methods. These use local kernel methods instead of a single global distribution model. This type of method tries to combine parametric and non parametric methods.

2.7 Conclusion

We have introduced two classification schemes for outlier detection: data miners and statisticians have different understandings of this problem. Outlier detection is a complex topic and there is no unique way to classify it. Our opinion about this is "it's not the color of the cat, what matters are it should be capable of catching mice." No matter which method we use, the key point is we can catch the outliers. So, let us introduce our outlier detection algorithm in the next chapter.

CHAPTER 3

METHODOLOGY

This section of the thesis contains the proposed method. We integrated univariate analysis with k-means clustering algorithm to pre-process the data first and then to do the cluster analysis in order to minimise our objective function i.e. Sum of distances between all the points and centroid of all the clusters.

3.1 Univariate Outliers

Given a data set of n observations of a variable x, let $\bar{x}$ be the mean and let s be standard deviation of the data distribution. One observation is declared as an outlier if lies outside of the interval-

$$(\bar{x} - ks, \bar{x} + ks), \tag{3.1}$$

where the value of k is usually taken as 2 or 3. The justification of these values relies on the fact that assuming normal distribution one expects to have a 95% (99%, respectively) percent of the data on the interval centered in the mean with a semi-length equal to two (three, respectively) standard deviation. Also, one expects to have the whole data inside an interval centered at the mean and three standard deviations as semi-length. From equation (3.1), the observation x is considered an outlier if

$$\frac{|x - \bar{x}|}{s} > k, \tag{3.2}$$

The problem with the above criteria is that it assumes normal distribution of the data something that frequently does not occur. Furthermore, the mean and standard deviation are highly sensitive to outliers. Two types of outliers are distinguished: *mild outliers* and *extreme outliers*. An observation x is declared an *extreme outlier* if it lies outside of the interval $(Q_1 - 3 \times IQR, Q_3 + 3 \times IQR)$. Notice that the center of the interval is $(Q_1 + Q_3)/2$ and its radius is $3.5 \times IQR$, where $IQR = Q_3 - Q_1$ is called the *Interquartile Range* and can be considered a robust

19

estimator of variability which can replace s in equation (3.2). On the other hand, $(Q_1+Q_3)/2$ is a robust estimator of the center that can be used instead of x in equation (3.1). An observation x is declared *a mild outlier* if it lies outside of the interval $(Q_1-1.5\times IQR, Q_3+1.5\times IQR)$. The numbers 1.5 and 3 are chosen by comparison with a normal distribution. All major statistical software applications include boxplots among their graphical displays. Figure 3.1 shows the outliers detected through their boxplots of the features in the class 1 (*setosa*) of the very well known *Iris* dataset, which has 150 instances and three classes.

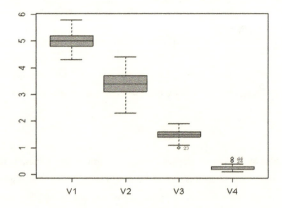

Figure.3.1. Outliers of the features in class 1 of the *Iris* data set

Using the same graphical display we detect as outliers the instance number 99 in the second class which has an abnormal value in the third feature and the instance 107 that has an abnormal value in the first feature of class 3.

3.1.1 Univariate Analysis

Univariate outliers are cases that have an unusual value for a single variable. One way to identify univariate outliers is to convert all of the scores for a variable to standard scores. Here we will calculate a z-score for the variable and then check for an outlier:

- If the sample size is small (80 or fewer cases), a case is an outlier if its standard score is ±2.5 or beyond.

- If the sample size is larger than 80 cases, a case is an outlier if its standard score is ±3.0 or beyond

This method applies to interval level variables, and to ordinal level variables that are treated as metric.

3.2 Multivariate Outliers

Let us consider a dataset D with p features and n instances. In a supervised classification context, we must also know the classes to which each of the instances belongs. It is very common to include the classes as the last column of the data matrix. The objective is to detect all the instances that seem to be unusual, these will be the multivariate outliers. One might think that multivariate outliers can be detected based on the univariate outliers in each feature, but as shown in the figure 2 this is not true. The instance appearing in the upper right corner is a multivariate outlier but it is not an outlier in each feature. On the other hand, an instance can have values that are outliers in several features but the whole instance might not be a multivariate outlier.

3.2.1 Multivariate Analysis

Multivariate analysis is performed on more than one variable. Similar to the univariate analysis a score is calculated here also based upon the Mahalanobis Distance. Mahalanobis D^2 is a multidimensional version of a z-score. It measures the distance of a case from the centroid (multidimensional mean) of a distribution, given the covariance (multidimensional variance) of the distribution. A case is a multivariate outlier if the probability associated with its $D^2 \leq 0.001$ D^2 follows a chi-square distribution with degrees of freedom equal to the number of variables included in the calculation. Mahalanobis D^2 requires that the variables be metric, i.e. interval level or ordinal level variables that are treated as metric.

21

3.3. Statistical Based Outlier Detection

Let x be an observation of a multivariate data set consisting of n observations and p features. Let x be the centroid of the dataset, which is a p-dimensional vector with the means of each feature as components. Let X be the matrix of the original dataset with columns centred by their means. Then the p×p matrix S=1/ (n-1) X'X represents the covariance matrix of the p features. The multivariate version of equation (3.3) is

$$D^2(x,\bar{x}) = (x-\bar{x})S^{-1}(x-\bar{x}) > k \tag{3.3}$$

as a Chi-Square distribution for a large number of instances. Therefore the proposed cut-off point in (3) is given by $k = \chi^2_{p,1-\alpha}$, where χ^2 stands for the Chi-Square distribution and α is a signification level usually taken as .05. A basic method for detecting multivariate outliers is to observe the outliers that appear in the box plot of the distribution of the Mahalanobis distance of the all instances. Looking at figure 3.2 we notice that only two outliers (instances 119 and 132) are detected in class 3 of the *Iris* dataset. People in the data mining community prefer to rank the instances using an outlyingness measures rather than to classify the instances in two types: outliers and non-outliers. Rocke and Woodruff (1996) stated that the Mahalanobis distance works well identifying scattered outliers.

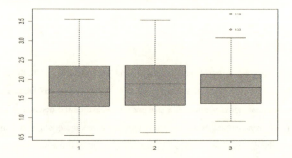

Figure.3.2 Boxplots of the Mahalanobis distances for each instance in the three classes of the *Iris* dataset

22

Equivalently after the deletion of one outlier, the other instance may emerge as an outlier. Masking occurs when a group of outlying points skews the mean and covariance estimates toward it, and the resulting distance of the outlying point from the mean is small..

3.4 Cluster Analysis to Check the Effects of Outlier

3.4.1. Problem Definition with Clustering

Clustering[35], or unsupervised classification, will be considered as a combination problem where the aim is to partition a set of *data object* into a predefined number of clusters. Number of clusters might be found by means of the *cluster validity criterion* or defined by user. Data object, *feature vector* and *attribute* are shown in Figure 1.6. The attributes of an object can be represented by a feature vector, where each element of the vector corresponds to one attribute. There are no examples that what kind of desirable relations should be valid among the data and that is why clustering is perceived as an unsupervised process. The objects with similar features should be grouped together and objects with different features placed in separate groups [25]. Dissimilarities are assessed based on the attribute values describing the objects. Often, distance measure between the two feature vectors is used to show dissimilarity between objects [30].

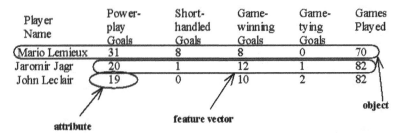

Player Name	Power-play Goals	Short-handled Goals	Game-winning Goals	Game-tying Goals	Games Played
Mario Lemieux	31	8	8	0	70
Jaromir Jagr	20	1	12	1	82
John Leclair	19	0	10	2	82

object

attribute   feature vector

Figure.3.3. Explanations for basic concepts.

3.4.2 Classification of Methods

Clustering algorithms can be classified according to the method adopted to define the individual clusters. The algorithms can be broadly classified into the following types: *partitional clustering, hierarchical clustering, density-based clustering* and *grid-based clustering* [29]. These algorithms are based on distance measure between two objects. Basically the goal is to minimize the distance of every object from the center of the cluster to which the object belongs.

3.4.2.1 Partitional Clustering

Partition-based methods construct the clusters by creating various partitions of the dataset. So, partition gives for each data object the cluster index *pi*. The user provides the desired number of clusters *M*, and some criterion function is used in order to evaluate the proposed partition or the solution. This measure of quality could be the average distance between clusters; for instance, some well-known algorithms under this category are *k-means, PAM* and *CLARA* [31]. One of the most popular and widely studied clustering methods for objects in Euclidean space is called *k-means clustering*. Given a set of N data objects x_i and an integer M number of clusters. The problem is to determine C, which is a set of M cluster representatives c_j, as to minimize the mean squared Euclidean distance from each data object to its nearest centroid. The algorithm starts with an initial solution and then involves an iterative scheme that operates over a fixed number of clusters, while a stopping criterion is met, i.e. the centers of the clusters stop changing. Algorithm contains simple steps as follows. Firstly, initial solution is assigned to random to the M sets:

$$c_j \leftarrow x_i | j = random(1, M), i = random(1, N) \qquad (3.4)$$

Then, in the first step, the data objects are partitioned as to each cluster centroid is closest to the data object in respect to the distance function:

$$p_i \leftarrow \arg\min d(x_i, c_j)^2 \forall i \in (1, N) \qquad (3.5)$$

24

In the second step, the cluster centroids are recalculated corresponding to the new partition:

$$c_j \leftarrow \frac{\sum\limits_{p_i=j} x_i}{\sum\limits_{p_i=j} 1} \forall j \in [1, M] \qquad (3.6)$$

The number of iterations depends upon the dataset, and upon the quality of initial clustering data. The k-means algorithm is very simple and reasonably effective in most cases. Completely different final clusters can arise from differences in the initial randomly chosen cluster centers. In final clusters k-means do not represent global minimum and it gets as a result the first local minimum. Main advantage of the k-means method is as follows: almost any solution not obtained by a k-means method can be improved. Disadvantage is that these methods only work well for finding clusters with spherical shapes and similar sizes.

3.5 K-Means Method

In data mining k-means algorithm is a method of cluster analysis which aims to partition n-observations into k-clusters in which each observation belongs to the cluster with the nearest mean. Unlike hierarchical clustering, k-means clustering operates on actual observations (rather than the larger set of dissimilarity measures), and creates a single level of clusters. The distinctions mean that k-means clustering is often more suitable than hierarchical clustering for large amounts of data. k- means treats each observation in your data as an object having a location in space. It finds a partition in which objects within each cluster are as close to each other as possible, and as far from objects in other clusters as possible. We can choose from five different distance measures, depending on the kind of data we are clustering. Each cluster in the partition is defined by its member objects and by its centroid, or center. The centroid for each cluster is the point to which the sum of distances from all objects in that cluster is minimized. k- means computes cluster centroids differently for each distance measure, to minimize the sum with respect to the measure that you specify. K-means uses an iterative algorithm that minimizes the sum of distances from each object to its cluster centroid, over all clusters. This algorithm moves objects between clusters until the sum cannot be decreased further. The result is a set of clusters that are as compact and well-separated as possible. You can control the details of the minimization using several optional

25

input parameters to k-means, including ones for the initial values of the cluster centroids, and for the maximum number of iterations.

The k-mean [32] clustering algorithm partitions a dataset D into k clusters. The objective of the algorithm is to minimize the sum of distances from the observations in the clusters to their cluster means. Suppose we have a dataset D with n observations $\{X_1, X_2, \ldots, X_n\}$. Assume that we have D partitioned into k clusters $C_1, \ldots, C_k$ with the corresponding means μ_i, $i \in [1, k]$. The objective function of the k-mean algorithm can be formally defined as follows:

$$\arg\min_{c_1 \ldots c_k} \sum_{i=1}^{k} \sum_{x_j \in c_i} \left\| X_j - u_i \right\|^2 \tag{3.7}$$

The k-mean algorithm consists of two steps: a clustering step and an update step. Initially, k distinct cluster means are selected either randomly or heuristically. In the clustering step, the k-mean algorithm clusters the dataset using the current k cluster means. A cluster C_i is a set that consists of all the observations X_j such that:

$$C_i = \{X_j \in D \mid \min_{l \in [1,k]} \left\| X_j - u_l \right\|^2\} \tag{3.8}$$

In the update step, the cluster means are updated as follows:

$$u_i = \frac{\sum X_j}{|C_i|}, \forall X_j \in C_i \tag{3.9}$$

The *k*-means algorithm is run multiple times until the means converge or until the number of iterations is greater than a chosen threshold NΘ. In general, the k-mean algorithm is very efficient. However, the number of clusters depends on the parameter k. In addition, the k-mean algorithm is not designed to detect clusters with different densities and shapes [32]

After getting an introduction of both the univariate analysis and k-means algorithm now we introduce the proposed algorithm as follows:

3.6 Proposed Algorithm

Step 1: Choose a dataset.

Step 2: Apply Univariate Outlier Detection to do the pre-processing of data before applying cluster analysis.

Step 3: If Outlier is detected based upon the criterion

- If the sample size is small (80 or fewer cases), a case is an outlier if its standard score is ±2.5 or beyond.

- If the sample size is larger than 80 cases, a case is an outlier if its standard score is ±3.0 or beyond

Then run the k-means (clustering) algorithm, for the dataset with and without the tuple having outlier, using replicates in order to select proper centroids so as to overcome the problem of local minima.

Step 4: Compare the results for the sum of point-to-centroid distances. The main goal of k-means algorithm is to find the clusters in such a way so as to minimize the sum of point to centroid distance.

Step 5: If Sum (without outlier) < Sum (with outlier), then remove the tuple having outlier permanently from the dataset.

Flowchart is given below for the proposed algorithm.

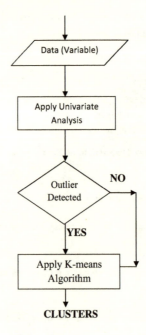

Figure.3.4 Flowchart of the proposed algorithm

CHAPTER 4

EXPERIMENTAL RESULTS

We used two different datasets here, one hypothetical data has been made by introducing some outlier values in the well known fisheriris data, having four features namely sepal length, sepal width, petal length, petal width and 150 tuples and two other datasets and other one is GSS93 dataset.

4.1 Dataset1

4.1.1 Univariate Analysis

After selecting the dataset we applied Univariate outlier detection on it using statistical approach as we defined in chapter 3. Results of the univariate outlier analysis are shown in Figure.4.1. Firstly we draw a scatter plot here between the two variables or our dataset which are susceptible to the outlier. With the help of the scatter plot we get to know the outlier point if any in the dataset. An outlier is usually a point which is far apart from other points of the dataset. Here the point encircled with red color is the outlier.

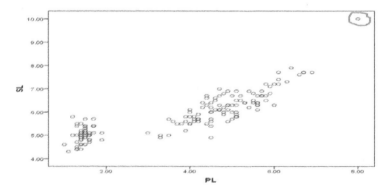

Figure.4.1.Plot between sepal length and petal length in the presence of outlier

The plot shows the distribution of points between the two features of our data Sepal length and Petal length, and the highlighted point in red circle shows the outlier point. After getting an idea about the outlier we will perform the univariate descriptive analysis and hence generate a score which here is a z-score and once we got the scores we will check for the entries with $3 < z\text{-score} < -3$, if there are any such entries we will remove those entries from our original variable. The descriptive univariate analysis applied on sepal length feature of the data (with outlier) gives following results, shown in Table.4.1, whereas that of analysis of data (without outlier) is shown in Table.4.2.

Table 4.1. Descriptive univariate analysis of the data (with outlier) for dataset1

Descriptive Statistics

	N	Minimum	Maximum	Mean	Std. Deviation
SL	151	4.30	10.00	5.8709	.89193
Valid N (listwise)	151				

Table 4.2. Descriptive univariate analysis of data (without outlier) for dataset1

Descriptive Statistics

	N	Minimum	Maximum	Mean	Std. Deviation
SL	150	4.30	7.90	5.8433	.82807
Valid N (listwise)	150				

We can easily observe here that the mean calculated in Table.4.1 is 5.8709 and the maximum value is 10 i.e. much greater than the mean whereas in Table.4.2.its nearer to the mean. We arrange the z-scores in ascending and descending order and hence search for any value lesser than -3 or greater than +3. Here we get a value greater than +3 when we arranged the z-scores in descending order, value shown in Table.4.3.

30

Table 4.3. Values of z-score, showing value > +3

1 : SL	10.0				
	SL	SW	PL	PW	ZSL
1	10.00	7.00	8.00	5.00	4.62943
2	7.90	3.80	6.40	2.00	2.27499
3	7.70	3.80	6.70	2.20	2.05076
4	7.70	2.80	6.70	2.00	2.05076
5	7.70	2.60	6.90	2.30	2.05076
6	7.70	3.00	6.10	2.30	2.05076

Now we must delete the outlier entry and save both the dataset i.e. with outlier entry and without outlier entry and run further the k-means algorithm to do the cluster analysis of the data and calculate the sum of points to centroid value in each case. After calculating both the values we will compare them to check whether the presence of outlier increases the sum or not, if it increases then it must be removed.

4.1.2 Results with K-Means Algorithm

4.1.2.1 Data without Outlier

k-means algorithm will now be executed to do the cluster analysis, here we will do the cluster analysis with two and three clusters respectively and will show the results of both the two. We have initially plotted the Silhouette values for both the values of k and based upon the observation we perform the clustering and compare the value of sum of point to centroid distance of all the clusters. Figure.4.2 shows the result for clustering performed with the value of $k = 2$.

31

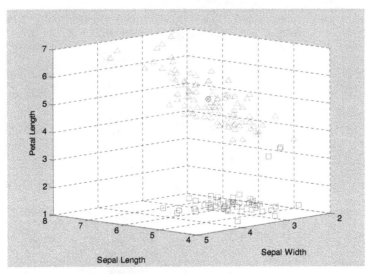

Figure.4.2 Cluster Analysis of Data with $k = 2$

Points in red and blue are the points of dataset, centroid of each cluster is shown in the figure by white coloured encircled 'x'

Now, we will further calculate the value of sum, Figure 4.3 shows the result for the value of sum when $k = 2$.

```
sum(sum2)
  iter    phase         num              sum
   1         1           150            243.76
   2         1            20            169.792
   3         1             6            153.232
   4         1             1            152.348
   5         2             0            152.348
5 iterations, total sum of distances = 152.348
4 iterations, total sum of distances = 152.348
4 iterations, total sum of distances = 152.348
6 iterations, total sum of distances = 152.348
4 iterations, total sum of distances = 152.348
7 iterations, total sum of distances = 152.348
3 iterations, total sum of distances = 152.348
6 iterations, total sum of distances = 152.348
7 iterations, total sum of distances = 152.348
4 iterations, total sum of distances = 152.348
6 iterations, total sum of distances = 152.348

ans =

152.3480
```

Figure .4.3 Value of Sum of Point to Centroid Distance (k = 2)

Further we will see the results of cluster analysis when $k = 3$, figure .4.4 shows the results

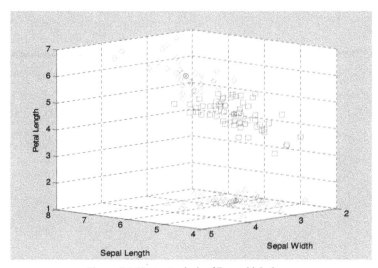

Figure .4.4 Cluster Analysis of Data with k=3

Now, we will further calculate the value of sum, Figure 4.5 shows the result for the value of sum when $k = 3$.

```
iter    phase       num           sum
  1       1         150        181.828
  2       1          23         92.2739
  3       1           7         80.4678
  4       1           3         79.054
  5       1           1         78.8514
  6       2           0         78.8514
 6 iterations, total sum of distances = 78.8514
 7 iterations, total sum of distances = 78.8514
 6 iterations, total sum of distances = 78.8514
 5 iterations, total sum of distances = 78.8514
 6 iterations, total sum of distances = 142.754
 5 iterations, total sum of distances = 78.8514
 7 iterations, total sum of distances = 78.8514
16 iterations, total sum of distances = 78.8514
 5 iterations, total sum of distances = 78.8514
 7 iterations, total sum of distances = 78.8514
12 iterations, total sum of distances = 78.8514

ans =

   78.8514
```

Figure .4.5 Value of Sum of Point to Centroid Distance ($k = 3$)

33

Value of sum comes out to be 78.8514 when we took $k = 3$.

4.1.2.2 Data with Outlier

Similar to the previous section now we will perform the cluster analysis on the data in which outlier entries have been introduced. Figure .4.6 shows the results of clustering done with $k = 2$.

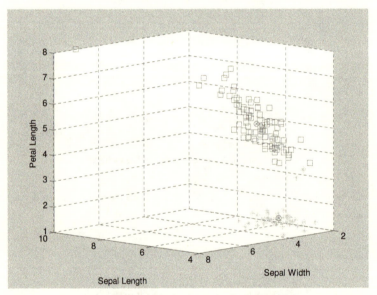

Figure .4.6 Cluster Analysis of Data (outlier) with k=2

Now, we will further calculate the value of sum, Figure 4.7 shows the result for the value of sum when $k = 2$.

```
sum(sumd2)
  iter    phase       num              sum
    1        1         150           288.01
    2        1          17          228.541
    3        1           8          204.194
    4        1           2           201.91
    5        2           0           201.91
5 iterations, total sum of distances = 201.91
4 iterations, total sum of distances = 201.91
4 iterations, total sum of distances = 201.91
6 iterations, total sum of distances = 201.91
4 iterations, total sum of distances = 201.91
5 iterations, total sum of distances = 201.91
3 iterations, total sum of distances = 201.91
5 iterations, total sum of distances = 201.91
6 iterations, total sum of distances = 201.91
4 iterations, total sum of distances = 201.91
6 iterations, total sum of distances = 201.91

ans =

  201.9098
```

Figure .4.7 Value of Sum (outlier) of Point to Centroid Distance ($k = 2$)

Further we will see the results of cluster analysis when k=3, figure .4.8 shows the results

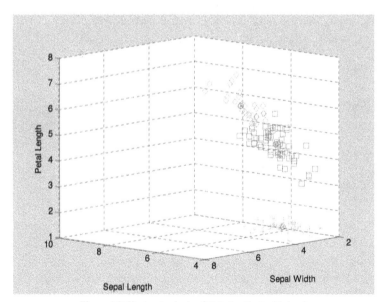

Figure 4.8 Cluster Analysis of Data (outlier) with $k = 3$

Now, we will further calculate the value of sum, Figure 4.9 shows the result for the value of sum when $k = 3$.

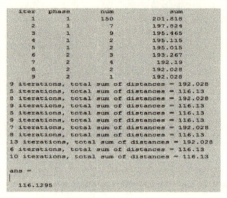

iter	phase	num	sum
1	1	150	201.818
2	1	7	197.824
3	1	9	195.465
4	1	2	195.115
5	1	2	195.015
6	2	3	193.267
7	2	4	192.19
8	2	2	192.028
9	2	1	192.028

```
9 iterations, total sum of distances = 192.028
5 iterations, total sum of distances = 116.13
8 iterations, total sum of distances = 192.028
9 iterations, total sum of distances = 116.13
5 iterations, total sum of distances = 116.13
9 iterations, total sum of distances = 116.13
7 iterations, total sum of distances = 192.028
8 iterations, total sum of distances = 116.13
13 iterations, total sum of distances = 192.028
6 iterations, total sum of distances = 116.13
10 iterations, total sum of distances = 116.13

ans =

116.1295
```

Figure .4.9 Value of Sum (outlier) of Point to Centroid Distance ($k = 3$)

As of now we have all the results, so we can now perform a comparison of the results we achieved in the previous two sections. Table 4.4 shows the comparison for the value of sum came out after applying the proposed method for value of $k = 2$ and 3 respectively.

Table 4.4 Comparison of the value of Sum

DATASET	Value of Sum (without Outlier)		Value of Sum (with Outlier)	
	K=2	K=3	K=2	K=3
Dataset 1	152.3480	78.8514	201.9098	116.1295

Value of the sum of all points in the cluster to the centroid comes out to be lesser when $k = 3$, and secondly value of sum is always lesser for the dataset without outlier entries. Hence we will delete the outlier entry permanently from the dataset, because this entry is not at all useful and distorting our original dataset by affecting our objective function.

4.2 Dataset2

4.2.1 Univariate Analysis

We will perform the univariate descriptive analysis and hence generate a score which here is a z-score and once we got the scores we will check for the entries with 3<z-score<-3, if there are any such entries we will remove those entries from our original variable. The descriptive univariate analysis applied on education (educ) feature of the data (with outlier) gives following results, shown in Table 4.5, where as that of analysis of data (without outlier) is shown in Table 4.6.

Table 4.5 Descriptive univariate analysis of the data (with outlier) for dataset2

	N	Minimum	Maximum	Mean	Std. Deviation
HIGHEST YEAR OF SCHOOL COMPLETED	2808	0	20	13.26	2.869
Valid N (listwise)	2808				

Table 4.6 Descriptive univariate analysis of the data (with outlier) for dataset2

	N	Minimum	Maximum	Mean	Std. Deviation
HIGHEST YEAR OF SCHOOL COMPLETED	2783	6	20	13.35	2.732
Valid N (listwise)	2783				

We can easily observe here that the mean calculated in Table.4.5. is 13.26 ,maximum value is 20 and minimum value is 6 i.e. much variation than the mean whereas in Table.4.6.variation is comparatively less. We arrange the z-scores in ascending and descending order and hence search for any value lesser than -3 or greater than +3. Here we get a value greater than +3 when we arranged the z-scores in descending order, value shown in Table.4.7.

Table 4.7 Values of z-score, showing value > +3

1 : Zeduc											
	sexprtyr	sibs	socbar	trust	tvhours	usblk	ushisp	wordsum	wrkslf	wwwhr	xmarsex	Zeduc
10		8	4	0	3	-1	-1	1	2	-1	2	-4.62307
11		16	7	9	12	-1	-1	4	2	-1	0	-3.92602
12		2	-1	2	-1	-1	-1	3	2	-1	1	-3.92602
13	0.35	6	4	2	2	20	998	-1	2	-1	0	-3.92602
14	0.02	0	-1	1	-1	-1	-1	10	1	5	8	-3.57749
15		0	-1	2	-1	999	999	-1	2	-1	1	-3.57749
16	0.00	3	6	8	98	45	43	-1	2	-1	0	-3.57749
17	0.10	7	-1	2	-1	998	998	-1	2	-1	3	-3.57749
18	0.02	5	7	0	4	-1	-1	2	0	-1	2	-3.57749
19	0.03	10	7	2	5	999	999	-1	2	-1	0	-3.57749
20	0.77	8	7	2	4	75	50	-1	0	-1	0	-3.22896
21		13	-1	2	-1	-1	-1	3	2	-1	1	-3.22896
22		14	6	9	2	-1	-1	99	2	-1	0	-3.22896
23	0.04	9	7	0	99	998	998	-1	2	-1	1	-3.22896
24	0.01	6	7	0	2	998	998	-1	2	-1	1	-3.22896
25	0.02	2	7	0	1	-1	-1	2	2	-1	1	-3.22896
26	0.03	4	-1	3	-1	50	40	-1	1	-1	8	-2.88044

Now we must delete the outlier entry and save both the dataset i.e. with outlier entry and without outlier entry and run further the k-means algorithm to do the cluster analysis of the data and calculate the sum of points to centroid value in each case. After calculating both the values we will compare them to check whether the presence of outlier increases the sum or not, if it increases then it must be removed.

4.2.2 Results with K-Means Algorithm

4.2.2.1 Data without Outlier

k- means algorithm will now be executed to do the cluster analysis, here we will do the cluster analysis with two and three clusters respectively and will show the results of both the two. We have initially plotted the Silhouette values for both the values of k and based upon the observation we perform the clustering and compare the value of sum of point to centroid distance of all the clusters. Figure.4.10 shows the result for clustering performed with the value of $k = 2$.

38

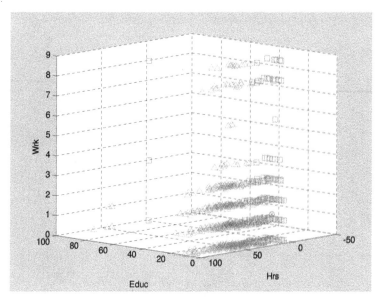

Figure 4.10 Cluster Analysis of Dataset2 with k = 2

Points in red and blue are the points of dataset, centroid of each cluster is shown in the figure by white coloured encircled 'x'. Now, we will further calculate the value of sum, Figure 4.11 shows the result for the value of sum when $k = 2$.

```
sum(sumd2)
iter    phase      num           sum
  1       1        2792      1.61265e+006
  2       1        1044        377929
  3       1          29        367260
  4       1           4        367185
  5       2           0        367185
5 iterations, total sum of distances = 367185
6 iterations, total sum of distances = 367185
4 iterations, total sum of distances = 367185
4 iterations, total sum of distances = 367185
3 iterations, total sum of distances = 367185
7 iterations, total sum of distances = 367185
6 iterations, total sum of distances = 367185
4 iterations, total sum of distances = 367185
4 iterations, total sum of distances = 367185
3 iterations, total sum of distances = 367185
5 iterations, total sum of distances = 367185

ans =

3.6719e+005
```

Figure .4.11 Value of Sum of Point to Centroid Distance (k = 2)

Further we will see the results of cluster analysis when $k = 3$, figure .4.12 shows the results

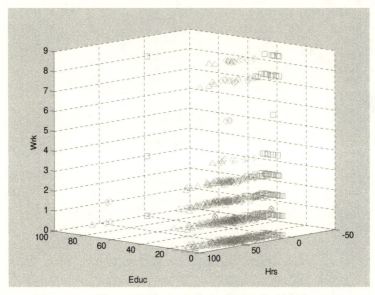

Figure 4.12 Cluster Analysis of Dataset2 with k=3

Now, we will further calculate the value of sum, Figure 4.13 shows the result for the value of sum when k=3.

```
5 iterations, total sum of distances = 289000
10 iterations, total sum of distances = 223633
6 iterations, total sum of distances = 228465
5 iterations, total sum of distances = 289000
6 iterations, total sum of distances = 228465
5 iterations, total sum of distances = 229743
7 iterations, total sum of distances = 228465
10 iterations, total sum of distances = 223633
3 iterations, total sum of distances = 228465
6 iterations, total sum of distances = 223633
4 iterations, total sum of distances = 306249

ans =

   2.2363e+005
```

Figure .4.13 Value of Sum of Point to Centroid Distance ($k = 3$)

4.2.2.2 Data with Outlier

Similar to the previous section now we will perform the cluster analysis on the data in which outlier entries have been introduced. Figure .4.6 shows the results of clustering done with $k = 2$.

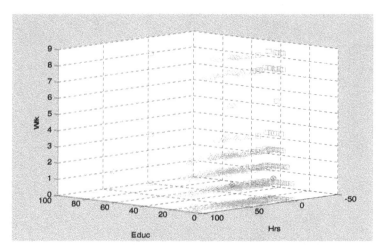

Figure 4.14 Cluster Analysis of Data (outlier) with k=2

Now, we will further calculate the value of sum, Figure 4.15 shows the result for the value of sum when $k = 2$.

```
sum (sumd2)
iter    phase      num          sum
  1       1        2517     1.6551e+006
  2       1        1096        382996
  3       1          54        370056
  4       1           4        369985
  5       2           0        369985
5 iterations, total sum of distances = 369985
4 iterations, total sum of distances = 369985
4 iterations, total sum of distances = 369985
6 iterations, total sum of distances = 369985
6 iterations, total sum of distances = 369985
4 iterations, total sum of distances = 369985
6 iterations, total sum of distances = 369985
5 iterations, total sum of distances = 369985
5 iterations, total sum of distances = 369985
5 iterations, total sum of distances = 369985
6 iterations, total sum of distances = 369985

ans =

3.6998e+005
```

Figure .4.15 Value of Sum (outlier) of Point to Centroid Distance ($k = 2$)

41

Further we will see the results of cluster analysis when $k = 3$, figure .4.16 shows the results

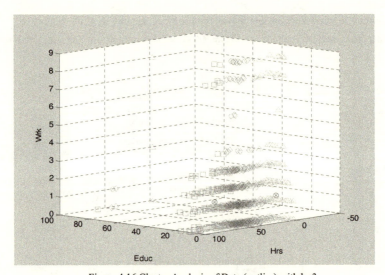

Figure 4.16 Cluster Analysis of Data (outlier) with k=3

Now, we will further calculate the value of sum, Figure 4.17 shows the result for the value of sum when $k = 3$.

iter	phase	num	sum
1	1	2817	227896
2	1	15	226319
3	1	1	226314
4	1	1	226312
5	2	0	226312

```
5 iterations, total sum of distances = 226312
10 iterations, total sum of distances = 226312
10 iterations, total sum of distances = 291784
9 iterations, total sum of distances = 231133
5 iterations, total sum of distances = 231133
7 iterations, total sum of distances = 226312
7 iterations, total sum of distances = 291784

ans =

2.2631e+005
```

Figure .4.17 Value of Sum (outlier) of Point to Centroid Distance ($k = 3$)

As of now we have all the results, so we can now perform a comparison of the results we achieved in the previous two sections. Table 4.4 shows the comparison for the value of sum came out after applying the proposed method for value of $k = 2$ and 3 respectively.

Table 4.8 Comparison of the value of Sum

DATASET	Value of Sum (without Outlier)		Value of Sum (with Outlier)	
	K=2	K=3	K=2	K=3
Dataset 1	3.6719e+005	2.2363e+005	3.6998e+005	2.2631e+005

CHAPTER 5

CONCLUSION AND FUTURE WORK

The conclusion of the whole report lies in the fact that outliers are usually the unwanted entries which always affects the data in one or the other form and distorts the distribution of the data. Sometimes it becomes necessary to keep even the outlier entries because they play an important role in the data but in our case as we are achieving our main objective i.e. to minimize the value of the sum by choosing optimum centroids, we will delete the outlier entries.

In our analysis we observed that for both the datasets the clustering results are better for the outlier less data as the value of the objective function i.e. 'SUM' gets minimized when we perform clustering on the outlier less data and increases in the presence of outlier. We produce a table here for representing the results of both the datasets and their values of sum of points to centroid distance in all clusters.

In future, the datasets where the outliers can be present in multiple variables can be used to do the same kind of analysis by using multivariate analysis and k-means or any other clustering algorithm or classification algorithm like k-nearest neighbor search etc.

REFERENCES

[1]. Williams, Graham, Rohan Baxter, Hongxing He, Simon Hawkins, and Lifang Gu. "A comparative study of RNN for outlier detection in data mining." In Data Mining, 2002. ICDM 2003. Proceedings. 2002 IEEE International Conference on, pp. 709-712. IEEE, 2002.

[2]. Han, Jiawei, Micheline Kamber, and Jian Pei. Data mining: concepts and techniques. Morgan kaufmann, 2006.

[3]. Markou, Markos, and Sameer Singh. "Novelty detection: a review—part 1: statistical approaches." Signal processing 83, no. 12 (2003): 2481-2497.

[4]. Ohsawa, Yukio, and Peter McBurney. "Chance discovery (Advanced information processing)." (2003): 2-15.

[5]. Ghosh-Dastidar, Bonnie, and J. L. Schafer. "Outlier detection and editing procedures for continuous multivariate data." JOURNAL OF OFFICIAL STATISTICS-STOCKHOLM- 22, no. 3 (2006): 487.

[6]. Guha, Sudipto, Rajeev Rastogi, and Kyuseok Shim. "ROCK: A robust clustering algorithm for categorical attributes." Information systems 25, no. 5 (2000): 345-366.

[7]. Phua, Clifton, Damminda Alahakoon, and Vincent Lee. "Minority report in fraud detection: classification of skewed data." ACM SIGKDD Explorations Newsletter 6, no. 1 (2004): 50-59.

[8]. Hodge, Victoria, and Jim Austin. "A survey of outlier detection methodologies."Artificial Intelligence Review 22, no. 2 (2004): 85-126.

[9]. Ester, Martin, Hans-Peter Kriegel, Jörg Sander, and Xiaowei Xu. "A density-based algorithm for discovering clusters in large spatial databases with noise." Kdd, 1996.

[10]. Breunig, Markus M., Hans-Peter Kriegel, Raymond T. Ng, and Jörg Sander. "LOF: identifying density-based local outliers." In ACM Sigmod Record, vol. 29, no. 2, pp. 93-104. ACM, 2000.

[11]. Knox, Edwin M., and Raymond T. Ng. "Algorithms for mining distance-based outliers in large datasets." In Proceedings of the International Conference on Very Large Data Bases. 1998.

[12]. Knorr, Edwin, and Raymond Ng. "Finding intensional knowledge of distance-based outliers." In Proceedings of the International Conference on Very Large Data Bases, pp. 211-222. 1999.

[13]. Knorr, Edwin M., and Raymond T. Ng. "A unified notion of outliers: Properties and computation." In Proc. KDD, vol. 1997, pp. 219-222. 1997.

[14]. Kollios, George, Dimitrios Gunopulos, Nick Koudas, and Stefan Berchtold. "Efficient biased sampling for approximate clustering and outlier detection in large data sets." Knowledge and data engineering, ieee transactions on 15, no. 5 (2003): 1170-1187.

[15]. Kriegel, Hans-Peter, and Arthur Zimek. "Angle-based outlier detection in high-dimensional data." In Proceedings of the 14th ACM SIGKDD international conference on Knowledge discovery and data mining, pp. 444-452. ACM, 2008.

[16]. Johnson, Theodore, Ivy Kwok, and Raymond Ng. "Fast computation of 2-dimensional depth contours." In Proc. KDD, vol. 1998, pp. 224-228. 1998.

[17]. Chapra, Steven C., and Raymond Canale. Numerical methods for engineers. McGraw-Hill, Inc., 2005.

[18]. Bilen, Canan, and S. Huzurbazar. "Wavelet-based detection of outliers in time series." Journal of Computational and Graphical Statistics 11, no. 2 (2002): 311-327.

[19]. Liu, Huan, and Lei Yu. "Toward integrating feature selection algorithms for classification and clustering." Knowledge and Data Engineering, IEEE Transactions on 17, no. 4 (2005): 491-502.

[20]. Bouguessa, Mohamed, and Shengrui Wang. "Mining projected clusters in high-dimensional spaces." Knowledge and Data Engineering, IEEE Transactions on 21, no. 4 (2009): 507-522.

[21]. Alfuraih, Saleh I., Nien T. Sui, and Dennis McLeod. "Using trusted email to prevent credit card frauds in multimedia products." World Wide Web 5, no. 3 (2002): 245-256.

[22]. Lazarevic, Aleksandar, Levent Ertoz, Vipin Kumar, Aysel Ozgur, and Jaideep Srivastava. "A comparative study of anomaly detection schemes in network intrusion detection." In Proceedings of the third SIAM international conference on data mining, vol. 3, pp. 25-36. Siam, 2003.

[23]. Liu, Jinhui, and Paul Gader. "Neural networks with enhanced outlier rejection ability for off-line handwritten word recognition." Pattern Recognition 35, no. 10 (2002): 2061-2071.

[24]. Aggarwal, Charu C., and Philip S. Yu. "Redefining clustering for high-dimensional applications." Knowledge and Data Engineering, IEEE Transactions on 14, no. 2 (2002): 210-225.

[25]. Fränti, Pasi, and Juha Kivijärvi. "Randomised local search algorithm for the clustering problem." Pattern Analysis & Applications 3, no. 4 (2000): 358-369.

[26]. Halkidi, Maria, Yannis Batistakis, and Michalis Vazirgiannis. "Clustering algorithms and validity measures." In Scientific and Statistical Database Management, 2001. SSDBM 2001. Proceedings. Thirteenth International Conference on, pp. 3-22. IEEE, 2001.

[27]. Halkidi, Maria, Yannis Batistakis, and Michalis Vazirgiannis. "Cluster validity methods: part I." ACM Sigmod Record 31, no. 2 (2002): 40-45.

[28]. Halkidi, Maria, Yannis Batistakis, and Michalis Vazirgiannis. "Clustering validity checking methods: part II." ACM Sigmod Record 31, no. 3 (2002): 19-27.

[29]. Paquet, Eric. "Exploring anthropometric data through cluster analysis." (2004).

[30]. Zhang, Yu-Fang, Jia-Li Mao, and Zhong-Yang Xiong. "An efficient clustering algorithm." In Machine Learning and Cybernetics, 2003 International Conference on, vol. 1, pp. 261-265. IEEE, 2003.

[31]. Vijendra, Singh, Laxman Sahoo, and Kelkar Ashwini. "An effective clustering algorithm for data mining." In Data Storage and Data Engineering (DSDE), 2010 International Conference on, pp. 250-253. IEEE, 2010.

[32]. MacQueen, James. "Some methods for classification and analysis of multivariate observations." In Proceedings of the fifth Berkeley symposium on mathematical statistics and probability, vol. 1, no. 281-297, p. 14. 1967.

[33]. Kim, Seung, Nam Wook Cho, Bokyoung Kang, and Suk-Ho Kang. "Fast outlier detection for very large log data." Expert Systems with Applications 38, no. 8 (2011): 9587-9596.

[34]. Chen, Shuyan, Wei Wang, and Henk van Zuylen. "A comparison of outlier detection algorithms for ITS data." Expert Systems with Applications 37, no. 2 (2010): 1169-1178.

[35]. Vijendra, Singh. "Efficient clustering for high dimensional data: Subspace based clustering and density based clustering." Information Technology Journal 10, no. 6 (2011): 1092-1105.

www.ingramcontent.com/pod-product-compliance
Lightning Source LLC
LaVergne TN
LVHW042349060326
832902LV00006B/489